We Speak Your Language

A Picture History to Commemorate the 90th
Anniversary of Central Library
Queens Public Library

1930-2020

Nelson Yusheng Lu

I Wing Press

Published by: I Wing Press, New York

www.iwingpress.com

Publisher: Paul Xinye Qiu

Design & layout: Changhua Wang

Nelson Yusheng Lu

We Speak Your Language: A Picture History to Commemorate the 90th Anniversary of Central Library, Queens Public Library 1930 – 2020 / Nelson Yusheng Lu. – First edition, February 2020.

ISBN 978-1-940742-49-6

1.   Queens Borough Public Library – History.

2.   Public libraries – United States – Pictorial works.

3.   Public libraries – New York (State) – New York – History.

027.47 – DC23

FOREWORD

For its first 34 years, Queen Public Library faced the challenge of meeting the educational needs of a population that exploded from about 150,000 in 1896 to 1.1 million in the 1920s. By then, this vital institution was operating 18 branches and two dozen satellites that served schools, hospitals and more across 109 square miles without a main headquarters.

The days of decentralization finally ended April 1, 1930 with the opening of a large, modern library at 89-14 Parsons Boulevard in the heart of bustling downtown Jamaica. Some 7,000 children and adults poured through the doors of the new Central Library that day to absorb the vast collection of fiction, non-fiction and reference books and newspapers and magazines.

"At last the earnest prayers of the friends of free educational opportunities of the Borough have been answered," Dr. Henry Stoesser, former president of the Library's board of trustees, wrote in his 1929 annual report to the City of New York as the elegant, four-story, Renaissance Revival building neared completion.

As the population of Queens and Library system continued to expand over the next three decades, so did the need for an even larger, more streamlined Central Library. In response to public entreaties once again, the City of New York constructed a brand-new building a few blocks away on Merrick Boulevard, and converted the Parsons Boulevard location into a courthouse, and later, an apartment complex.

Central Library now draws more than 1.2 million visitors each year seeking knowledge, information and a path to a better life. It continues to deliver for them, as it has since the day it originally opened 90 years ago.

I want to thank Central Library Director Nelson Lu for compiling this fascinating history of Central Library to honor its nine decades of service to the community, the borough of Queens and beyond.

Dennis M. Walcott
President and CEO
Queens Public Library

PREFACE

For 90 years, the Central Library of Queens Public Library has served the informational, recreational, cultural and recreational needs for the people of Queens. As the borough has grown and changed, so has our Central Library.

I have had the privilege of directly leading the team at the Central Library as the Associate Director from 2009-2012 and studied the library services we provided decades earlier and oversaw the changes we implemented for decades to come. I have witness the Central Library provide three distinct goals within its mission: serve as a main research/reference library for the county; support branch libraries with materials, staffing and a knowledge base of subject expertise; and the community library for the surrounding neighborhood. While the first two goals are traditional for all central libraries, the third goal is less traditional and has been critical for transforming our library.

For more than any time in its 90-year history, the Central Library serves the surrounding neighborhood. With collections and programming dedicated to the community and newest immigrant groups, customers not only have the advantage of resources of a Central Library but more importantly a library that reflects their neighborhood.

Today, the Central Library for Queens Public Library welcomes over 1.5 million people and transforms lives on each visit.

The Queens Public Library and its Central Library embraces our responsibility and looks forward to the continuing this high quality service though the rest of the 21st century.

Nick Buron
Chief Librarian
Queens Public Library

MISSION STATEMENT

Queens Public Library transforms lives by cultivating personal and intellectual growth and by building strong communities.

VISION

Our vision is a vibrant, informed, cohesive, and empowered society.

VALUES

Inclusion – Queens Public Library welcomes and serves everyone.

Access – We provide free information, programs, and services that are open to all.

Intellectual Freedom – We uphold the right to privacy and the right to seek, access, and express diverse points of view.

Customer Service – We care about the people we serve and strive to deliver exceptional experiences.

Innovation – We encourage organizational and staff innovation that adapts to emerging needs.

Integrity – We are committed to transparency and accountability.

Respect – We treat our customers, staff, and diverse communities with respect and courtesy.

Excellence – We hold ourselves to the highest standards in everything we do.

Contents

FOREWORD   I

PREFACE   II

MISSION STATEMENT   III

PART ONE
A Brief History of the Queens Public Library   1

    A: The Origin of Queens and the Queens Public Library   1

    B: A Brief History of Jamaica and Jamaica Branch & Colonial Hall   6

PART TWO
The First Central Library at Parsons Blvd. 1930 – 1966   9

    A: 1930 – 1940s   9

    B: 1950s – 1966   23

PART THREE
The New Central Library at Merrick Blvd. 1966 – Present   35

    A: 1966 – 1970s   35

    B: 1980s   43

    C: 1990s   50

    D: 2000s   64

    E: 2010s   86

PART FOUR
The Future of the Central Library   114

Appendix   125

    A: Directors/Chief Librarians/Presidents of Queens Public Library   125

    B: Managers/Directors of Central Library, Queens Public Library   126

PART ONE

A Brief History of the Queens Public Library

A: The Origin of Queens and the Queens Public Library

Queens County, one of the original counties in the English province of New York, was formed in 1683.

Brooklyn - Queens - Nassau Map, 1600s.

Queens County originally stretched east to Suffolk, encompassing the towns of Newtown, Flushing, Jamaica, Hempstead, and Oyster Bay. A year later, the township of Hempstead, North Hempstead, and Oyster Bay formed Nassau County. In January 1, 1898, the creation of the City of Greater New York fused Long Island City, Flushing, Newtown, Jamaica, and the Rockaways into the Borough of Queens, as part of New York City.

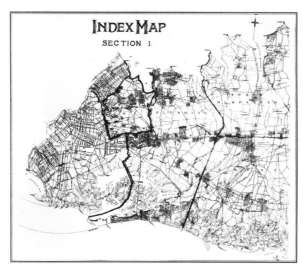

The Map of Queens County, E. Belcher Hyde, 1896.

The first public library in Queens was organized in 1858 in Flushing and it functioned on a subscription basis. In 1884, it became a free circulation library.

The Original Flushing Library Association, Building at Main Street, 1891.

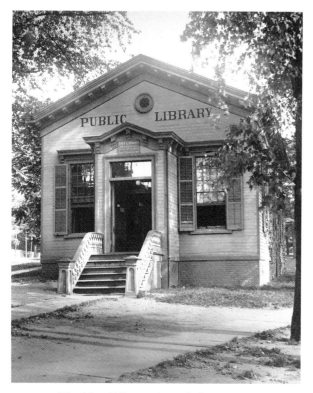

Flushing Library Association, 1906.

In the 1890s, several other communities had also started local library services. These included Steinway, Hollis, Queens Village, Richmond Hill, Ozone Park, Long Island City, and Astoria.

On March 19, 1896, Dr. Walter G. Frey and George E. Clay obtained a charter for the Long Island City Public Library. The Library opened the Nelson Branch in Hunters Point on August 3, 1896. Jessie Hume was the first librarian and became Chief Librarian in 1907.

The Steinway Free Circulating Library became the second branch in late 1896. Astoria Library, opened on Fulton Avenue, joined the Library in February 1898. On December 21, 1899, the Library was re-named the Queens Borough Library.

Dr. Walter. G. Frey, founded the Long Island City Public Library, and later become the President of the Board of Trustees of the Queens Public Library.

The revised charter of the Long Island City Public Library, changing the name of the institution to the Queens Borough Library, 1899.

Children in front of the Nelson Branch, 1910. Located in Hunter Point, near 101 East Avenue & 11 Street, the Nelson Branch opened in 1896 as the first branch of the Long Island City Public Library, which became the Queens Borough Library after re-charter in 1899. Nelson Branch is considered the first branch of the Queens Public Library.

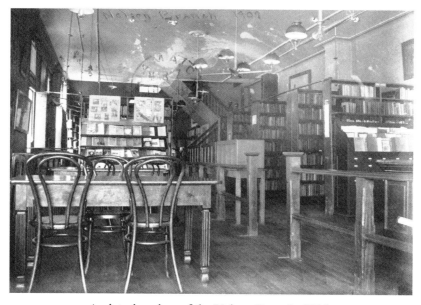

An interior view of the Nelson Branch, 1910.

The Steinway Free Circulating Library, 1896. It joined the Long Island City Public Library in late 1896 as its second branch.

The Long Island City Public Library opened a branch in Astoria at 112 Fulton Avenue on February 28, 1898. The third branch in the young system was the first to institute an open-shelf system.

In January 1901, shortly after the consolidation of Queens into New York City, the city government proposed a new charter joining all libraries in Queens into the Queens Public Library. Four of the community libraries were consolidated with the Queens Borough Library, including the Ozone Park Free Circulating Library, the Richmond Library, the Hollis Public Library, and the Queens Village Free Library. The charter granted to the new system by the Regents of the State of New York was worded to extend the service area of the old Long Island City Public Library to the entire borough. Operating funds were provided by the City of New York shortly after the formation of the system. In December, Flushing Library Association also joined the Library.

The Queens Public Library was incorporated in May 1907, changing its legal name from Queens Borough Library to the Queens Borough Public Library. On October 18, the City of New York transferred control of the Queens Libraries to a new, independent board of trustees, while maintaining responsibility for the system's financial support.

B: A Brief History of Jamaica and Jamaica Branch & Colonial Hall

Jamaica was a former town and capital of Queens County. On May 17, 1686, New York Governor Thomas Dongan issued a charter to the landowners of Jamaica. The Dongan Charter consolidated the various hamlets into the town of Jamaica and set its boundaries. In 1898, Queens became part of the City of New York, with Jamaica as the county seat.

The Dongan Charter, 1686.

The Jamaica Circulating Library was established on November 26, 1860, two years after the founding of the Flushing Library Association. It also functioned on a subscription basis. "Any person may become a subscriber to the Association by paying one dollar for which he shall be entitled to the use of the Library and reading rooms for one year."

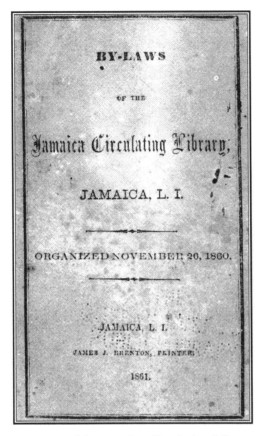

By-Laws of the Jamaica Circulating Library, 1860.

On November 1, 1906, the Queens Public Library opened the Jamaica branch at 22 Herriman Ave. (162th St.) with Miss Caroline Crysler as the librarian.

Since 1909, Jamaica had been rising in importance because of the Long Island Rail Road and the streetcar network, which extended into Brooklyn and Nassau. Stylish shops, office buildings, and movie theaters lined Jamaica Ave., which assumed greater importance in the life of the Queens borough.

Jamaica Railway Station near 152 Street, 1870.

South side of Jamaica Avenue, 1915.

Colonial Hall, 1909.

An interior view of the Colonial Hall, 1910.

In 1911, the Jamaica branch and administrative office moved to the building known as Colonial Hall, 402 Fulton Street. The Jamaica Branch and the Library Administration remained at this address until the sale of Colonial Hall in 1922. The branch was then moved to 330-32 Fulton Street and the administration to 150-24 Jamaica Ave.

Interior of the Central Building - Colonial Hall, the Reference and the Circulation desk, 1913.

PART TWO

The First Central Library at Parsons Blvd.
1930 – 1966

A: 1930 – 1940s

The construction of the Central Library at Parsons Blvd., 1928.

Central Library and the Queens Public Library administration needed a central building. In March 1926, the Library requested $345,000 for the construction of the Central Library in Jamaica. Departmentalization of the central building was in process and Central Reference Service had already been established in 1927. On October 23, 1928, the cornerstone-laying ceremony for the four-story Renaissance Revival Library on Parsons Blvd. took place. On November 1, 1929, the building was dedicated as the Central Library by Mayor James J. Walker.

On April 1, 1930, the new $1,000,000 Central Library building, the headquarters of the Queens Public Library, was opened to the public. More than 5,000 adults and nearly 2,000 children visited the new Central Library on its first opening day. The new centralized system of registration was put into effect on the same day. A central circulation system was also inaugurated where any branch would be able to draw on the literary resources of the Central Library.

The Jamaica Branch at Fulton Street and the Administration at Jamaica Avenue were moved to this new building.

Opening of the Central Library at Parsons Blvd., April 1, 1930.

The new Central Library at Parsons Blvd. included a Reference Division, Teachers' Reference Library, Children's Department, Foreign Collection, and Circulation Department. Included in the Reference Division was the Long Island Collection, which was formed in October 1911, and contained archival materials in regards to the Long Island geographical area.

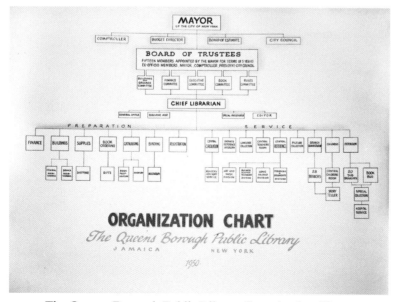

The Queens Borough Public Library Organization Chart.

Central Library children's room and its new murals, 1934.

Child reading book in the Central Library children's room, February 1936.

Juvenile/Children's Reading Room, 1940.

Central Circulation Charging Desk, September 1935.

Central Library Reference Division, 1935.

Long Island Collection, Central Library, October 1935.

The Central Library Adult Reading Room, March 1936.

Central Library Readers' Advisory Services, May 1937.

Central Library Picture Collection, 1939.

Central Library Art & Music Division, 1939.

The Periodical/Magazine Reading Room, 1939.

Central Library Foreign Language Collection, 1939.

Central Library's open bookshelves, 1934.

An art exhibition at Central Library, 1934.

Central Library, after blizzard, February 2, 1934.

Central Library display case – prize winning essay about constitution, September 22, 1937.

Storytime program at Central Library children's room, 1938.

Librarian helping customer at the Reference Division, April 1939.

Central Library "Christmas Tree" program, December 1939.

The "Adult Education Events" display at Central Library, April 1940.

The "America You Defend" exhibition and services at Central Library, 1945.

Band in front of the Central Library celebrating the 50th Anniversary of Queens Public Library, 1946.

Central Library "Book Week" program, 1949.

Despite the enthusiasm with which the new Central Library was opened, the Queens Public Library was not yet satisfied with the building. The Central Library building was expanded in the late of 1930s and early 1940s with WPA (Works Progress Administration) funds and added an 11-tier stack area. However, this only added operational complications and did nothing to relieve the cut-up nature of the building, nor did it provide the essential reader seating and open-shelf book stack space needed to serve a population which had grown to two millions in Queens.

Construction at Central Library, 1939.

The construction for the Central Library book stacks, July 1939.

Central Library exterior WPA sign, 1940.

B: 1950s – 1966

The Central Library had been flourishing. In the mid 1950s, new form of technology, microfiche and microfilm, appeared, and were welcomed by the patrons.

Street view of the Central Library at Parsons Blvd., January, 1950.

Customers using the microfilm reader for reading newspapers and magazines, 1960.

Customers returning books at Central Library Checking Desk, 1950.

The Travel Exhibition displayed outside the Central Library, 1952.

Central Library Adult Book Club, January 1952.

Children's Librarian conducted
program at children's room,
Central Library, 1953.

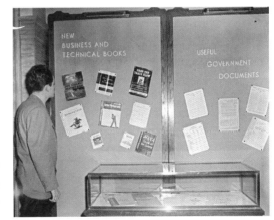

New book display at Business,
Science & Technology Division,
Central Library, March 1953.

Teachers studying at the
Teachers' Reference Library,
Central Library, March 1953.

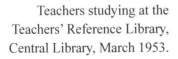

The Art and Music Division, Central Library, March 1953.

Customers reading magazines/newspapers at the Periodical Division, March 1953.

Central Library outdoor art show, June 1953.

The "Record Concert" program, June 1954.

Adult Educational Program, September 1954.

"Are you thinking about your future?"—The Library recruitment desk
at the main floor, Central Library, February 1955.

National Library Week event – Radio broadcast from Central Library, 1960.

An example of the overcrowded conditions, 1959.

With the growth of Queens and the Queens Public Library, the present Central Library was determined to be overcrowded and inadequate for the library needs of Queens.

In 1958, the City Council approved funding for planning and purchasing a site for a new Central Library. The Library proposed three possible sites: one on 89th Avenue between 162nd and 163rd Streets, one at the southeast corner of Parsons Boulevard and 90th Avenue, and one on Merrick Boulevard between 89th and 90th Avenues. In early February of 1960 the City Planning Commission chose the Merrick Boulevard site as its new Central Library site.

An example of the overcrowded conditions, 1959.

An example of the overcrowded conditions, 1959.

An example of the overcrowded conditions, 1959.

The Central Library site at Merrick Boulevard and 89 Avenue, as it looked in 1939.

On April 30, 1963, Mayor Robert F. Wagner approved contracts for the construction of a new Central Library building for the Queens Public Library in Jamaica. The new Central Library would cost an estimated $4.8 million, chargeable to capital funds, and would be erected on the easterly side of Merrick Blvd between 89 and 90 Avenue. On October 2, 1963, the excavation work of the new Central Library was officially approved by Queens Borough President Cariello. As of 1964, construction of the long awaited new Central Library on Merrick Blvd was right on schedule.

Architectural Drawing for new Central Library

An architectural drawing of the new Central Library, 1964.

The beginning of the construction for the new Central Library, 1963.

The construction site of Central Library, October 1963.

The Official Inspection Day, October 2, 1963. Left: QPL trustee Lornelius Hermann; Right: Chief Librarian Harold Tucker.

The new Central Library at Merrick Blvd under construction, 1964.

The new Central Library at Merrick Blvd under construction, 1964.

An interior view of the
new Central Library
under construction, 1965.

On March 14, 1966, the Central Library started its move from Parsons Blvd. to the new Central Library at Merrick Blvd. On March 21, 1966, the 36-year-old Central Library at Parsons Blvd. was closed to the public completely.

NEW CENTRAL LIBRARY GOES UNDER CONSTRUCTION

LOOKING OVER THE BUILDING PLANS

FRONT ROW: MEYER F. WILES, DEPUTY
COMMISSIONER OF PUBLIC WORKS, WITH
CORNELIUS B. HERRMANN, PRESIDENT,
BOARD OF TRUSTEES.

STANDING: TRUSTEES ROBERT GROH AND
DR. JOHN E. LOWRY, WITH BOROUGH
PRESIDENT MARIO J. CARIELLO AND
CHIEF LIBRARIAN.

FACT SHEET ON NEW CENTRAL BUILDING

LOCATION: 89-11 Merrick Blvd. (166th St.) between 89th & 90th Aves.

Building will face Merrick Blvd., with main entrance in center of block; on 90th Ave. a secondary entrance for children will be provided.

PLOT OF LAND: 69,200 sq. ft.

BUILDING:

Construction: Reinforced concrete with exterior walls of face brick trimmed with granite & limestone

Total Floor Area: 195,000 sq. ft. with capacity for 860,000 vols.

Cost (Total): $5,201,000

Construction work:	$3,968,000
Land cost:	318,000
Equipment & Furniture:	400,000
Books:	250,000
Architects' fees:	265,000

HISTORY: Replaces 32 year old Central Building on Parsons Boulevard

SPECIAL FEATURE: 200 seat lecture hall

COMPLETION: Scheduled for 1965

CONTRASTS BETWEEN NEW & PRESENT BUILDINGS

	NEW	PRESENT
Book Capacity	860,000 vols.	350,000 vols.
Square Feet	195,000	75,000
Readers Seats	1,000	271

INSPECTING EXCAVATION PROGRESS

BOARD PRESIDENT CORNELIUS B. HERRMANN;
BOROUGH PRESIDENT MARIO J. CARIELLO;
DEPUTY COMMISSIONER MEYER F. WILES; AND
CHIEF LIBRARIAN.

The "Fact Sheet" of the new Central Library, 1964.

PART THREE

The New Central Library at Merrick Blvd.
1966 – Present

A: 1966 – 1970s

On April 11, 1966, the new Central Library of the Queens Public Library opened to the public. The new building was the result of the unwavering efforts of Library Director Harold Tucker. It was designed by the architects York & Sawyer, Kiff, Colean, Voss, and Souder. The new library building cost about $5,703,971 and is a two-story building, with a basement and sub-basement, that has a total floor area of 195,000 square feet. The total designed volume capacity is 860,000 volumes of materials.

The new Central Library at Merrick Blvd. opened to the public on April 19, 1966.

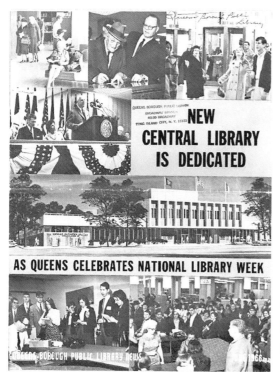

" New Central Library is
Dedicated" - Poster for the
grand opening, April 19, 1966.

Opening ceremony of the new Central Library, April 19, 1966. New York City
Mayor John Lindsay (second from right), QPL Chief Librarian Harold Tucker
(third from right), with other guests, cutting the ribbon in the ceremony.

People waiting outside for the grand opening, April 19, 1966.

The opening of the new Central Library, April 19, 1966.

New York City Mayor John Lindsay giving an address at the grand opening ceremony, April 19, 1966.

The Department of Sanitation Band playing in the grand opening ceremony, April 19, 1966.

Library staff helping customers on the grand opening day, April 19, 1966.

It was the first large urban library in the nation to provide all public services on one floor, with a seating of 1,000 for readers. The new library, in addition to main reading rooms and reference rooms, a lecture hall, public service areas, offices, meeting rooms, and other basic facilities, would have various special departments and collections, including a popular library, a student area, and rooms for children and young people. Subject services would include divisions for Art and Music, Science and Technology, Social Sciences, Language and Literature, History, Biography and Travel, and Long Island Division.

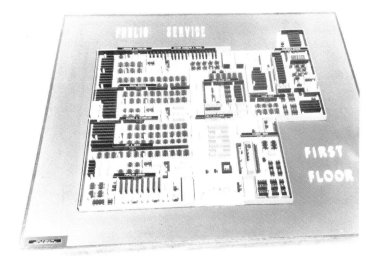

The model of the inside layout of the new Central Library, 1966.

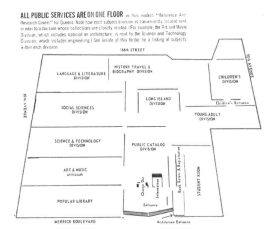

The floor plan of the new Central Library, 1966.

After grand opening, a visit to this new facility was one of the highlights of that year's American Library Association Convention in Manhattan. Delegates to the ALA Conference in New York that July would view the model of this modern, air-conditioned library at booth 701.

The model of the new Central Library for the ALA Annual Conference, 1966.

Bronze Plaque - Public Buildings
(Federal, State & City Financed)

CENTRAL BUILDING QUEENS BOROUGH PUBLIC LIBRARY

89-11 Merrick Boulevard, Jamaica

OF FIREPROOF two-story construction with reinforced concrete frame and floor, exterior of granite, limestone and face brick with aluminum windows, interior of exposed and plastered masonry block, acoustic tile ceilings, fluorescent lighting, vinyl asbestos tile floors, air-conditioned throughout, gross floor area: 194,300 square feet, major public service areas on first floor with two entrances, lecture room for 200, meeting and exhibit dual-purpose area in basement, administrative and technical processing division on second floor.

The new Central Library building received the 1965 Building Awards-Bronze Plaque, from the Chamber of Commerce of Queens.

In the late 1960s and mid-1970s, New York City faced a fiscal crisis, leading the City to request that the Queens Public Library implement a budget cut. Cuts in library services were a strategy of fiscal responsibility – with disastrous results. Library service citywide was brutally curtailed, with branches open only three days a week. However, Central Library still provided full services to Queens residents.

Children's Book Week at Center Library, 1974.

The Senior Citizens Convention at the Central Library, 1974.

"Library in Action" photo contest displaying at Central Library, 1974.

Associated Press wire services at Central Library, 1975.

Wednesday evening chess game at Central Library, January 11, 1978.

B: 1980s

While the Library continued to provide services for its customers, in 1982, the Library installed anti-theft devices in the Central Library and later in all branches.

In 1980s, new technology for the catalog was introduced. A computerized search catalog (CD-ROMs) supplanted the library card catalog for better accessing materials. And, to extend its services, the library was partially renovated and expanded in 1989.

African program at Central Library, 1980.

New York City Mayor Ed Koch (right) visited the Central Library, 1980.

Volunteer recognition ceremony, Central Library, 1985.

Central Library, child reading & the book display, 1988.

Central Library, customer browsing the computer bookshelves, 1988.

Customers searching the CD-ROM catalog at Central Library, April, 1988.

"This is the Library Catalog" - the new CD-ROM catalog replaced the card catalog, 1988.

Central Library window display: Marvin Bell - Window View, 1988.

Customers ready to check out books at the Central Circulation Services, 1988.

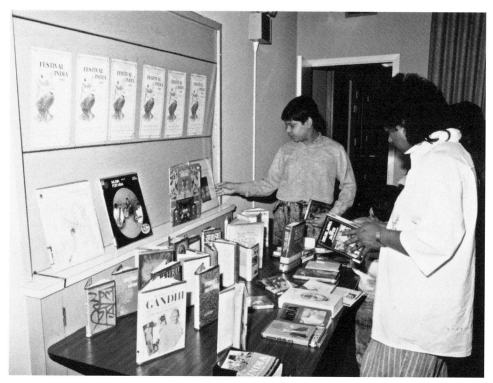

Book displays, 1989.

Indian dancing performance, Central Library, October 28, 1989.

Art & crafts program, 1989.

Central Library under partial renovation, 1989.

C: 1990s

The 1990s saw a truly successful renaissance in library building and services. In 1992, the circulation system was linked to a network of other, similar systems for exchanging cataloging records. The library's catalog became available on the Internet in May 1993. In October, the new Queens Public Library online catalog, titled "InfoLinQ" (Information Online at Queens Public Library) was unveiled at the Central Library.

Customer searching the Health Reference Center CD-ROM, which was installed in the Central Library in 1990.

Teens & the Teen Collections, 1990.

Civil War book discussion program, December 20, 1990.

Author Talk & book signing with Mr. Mark Mathabane, 1990.

Performance/program at the Children's Room, 1990.

Former First Lady Barbara Bush visiting the Central Library, September 4, 1991.

Former First Lady Barbara Bush joining the children's program at Central Library, September 4, 1991.

Summer Reading kickoff party, 1991.

Summer Reading club, 1991.

InfoLinQ was launched at Central Library, October 1993.

Customers using the InfoLinQ at Central Library, 1993.

New York City Mayor David Dinkins visiting the Central Library, celebrating 6 days service for the first time since 1947, 1993.

"Blueprint for change: the life and times of Lewis H. Latimer" exhibition at Central Library, 1995.

In 1995, the Library Gallery was established in the Central Library. In the same year, a grant from the National Endowment for the Humanities funded an exhibit about the life and work of the African American inventor Lewis Latimer - Civil War veteran, Flushing resident, and colleague of Thomas Edison. That was the first exhibit in the Central Library's new gallery, created to house cultural and historical exhibits. Many major exhibitions and events would be held in the Gallery incorporating historical and cultural themes in following years.

"Getting around: a history of transportation on Long Island" exhibition at Central Library, October 1997.

On March 19, 1996, the Library celebrated its 100th anniversary at the Central Library and branches. It was the day the Library entered cyberspace, unveiling its own home page on the World Wide Web (http://www.queens. lib.ny.us) and offering free public access to the Internet in the Central Library, a service later expanded to all branches. It permitted access to the Library's catalog, commercial research databases, fast links to select Internet sites and more. The catalog was available with English, Spanish, Chinese, and Korean interfaces.

The Board of Trustees and
Gary E. Strong, Director,
Queens Borough Public Library

Cordially invite you to attend
a special reception and sneak preview
of the new Centennial exhibit in the
Queens Library Gallery

Lighting the Way:
Queens Borough Public Library, 1896·1996

Historian and Curator
Jeffrey A. Kroessler, Ph.D.
will conduct private exhibit tours.

Monday, March 18, 1996   7:00 p.m.

Central Library
Second Floor, North Hall
89-11 Merrick Boulevard
Jamaica, New York 11432

Please R.S.V.P. by Monday, March 11
718/990-8665

The invitation of celebrating QPL Centennial at Central Library's Gallery, 1996.

New York City Mayor Rudolph
Giuliani speaking from the
podium at the Central Library
during the QPL Centennial
Celebration, March 19, 1996.

QPL Centennial Celebration at Central Library, March 19, 1996. NYC Mayor Rudolph Giuliani
(Left 3), Queens Borough President Claire Shulman (Left 5), and Library Director Gary Strong
(Right 2).

Flag banner parade passing the Central Library during the Centennial Celebration, March 19, 1996.

Clarinet band playing music on Central Library's main floor during the QPL Centennial Celebration, March 19, 1996.

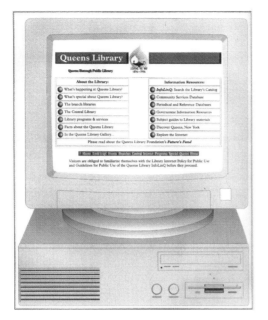

The new home page on the World Wide
Web --http://www.queens.lib.ny.us, 1996.

In January 1999 the new Cyber Center opened at the Central Library. The Cyber Center has 48 computers for customer use, allowing access to the Internet and word processing. The Cyber Center, along with additional computers in the library, has helped to close the gap between the technology "haves" and "have-nots" for Queens' residents.

The new Cyber Center at Central Library with customers, 1999.

Central Library staff helping a customer use the computer at the new Cyber Center, 1999.

Take Your Daughter to Work Day at Central Library, 1996.

Queens Borough President Claire Shulman joining the "Great New York Read Aloud" program, May 12, 1997.

Sesame Street (Muppet Zoe) at Central Library, August 17, 1997.

LL Cool J visiting the Central Library, October 15, 1997.

Central Library Current Collection –
New Books display, 1998.

"Festival Latino" program at Central Library, 1998.

Halloween costumes, 1999.

D: 2000s

Queens has been growing and becoming the most diverse place in America. The Central Library, QPL, is continuing to provide great customer services to its communities.

The exterior view of the Central Library, 2000.

"Gilded Rage" exhibition in Central Library, 2000.

"Flushing Remonstrance Display" at Central Library, 2000.

Young Adult Coordinator Nick Buron holding (right 2) a YA program at the Central Library Gallery, 2000.

American Legion donating books to the Children's Division, Central Library, 2000.

Children's program at the children room, Central Library, 2000.

Homework Help at Central Library, May 2000.

Art & Crafts program at Central Library, 2000.

Children's program at the Gallery, Central Library, December 2001.

Quilt making program at Central Library, 2001.

QPL Deputy Director Thomas Alford (Left) and Central Library Director Sherman Tang (Right) testing the new self-check-out machine, 2001.

Central Library celebrating MLK Day and Black History Month, January 2009.

To serve customers and better meet their needs, beginning in 2005, the Library undertook an ambitious project to expand and renovate the Central Library. The first phase of this project was the construction of a new children's library — the Children's Library Discovery Center. The construction began in 2008 and the Center officially opened to public in September 2011.

The site located in the corner of Merrick Blvd and 90 Avenue. The Library purchased the site and built the new Children's Library Discovery Center.

Children's Library Discovery Center under construction, 2009.

Discover-E, the Robot, announcing the grand opening of the Children's Library Discovery Center, September 15, 2011.

Queens Borough President Helen Marshall gave a speech at the grand opening ceremony of the new Children's Library Discovery Center, September 15, 2011.

Customers walking into the new Children's Library Discover Center in its grand opening ceremony, September 15, 2011.

The new Children's Library Discovery Center grand opening poster, September 2011.

The entrance of the new Children's Library Discovery Center, 2011.

The main lobby of the new Children's Library Discovery Center, 2011.

The interactive floor map of Queens, highlighting its neighborhoods and landmarks, 2011.

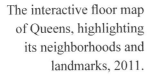
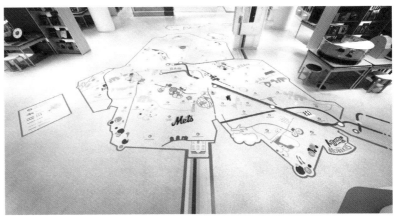

First floor, Children's Library Discovery Center, book and interactive exhibitions, 2011.

Second floor, Children's Library Discover Center, books and reading areas, 2011.

The signage in the Children's Library Discovery Center, 2011.

The Early Childhood Educational Center, the Children's Library Discovery Center, 2011.

The 500-gallon fish tank in the Children's Library Discovery Center, 2011.

The corner of the Children's Library Discovery Center, 2011.

The mini cyber center for children, located on second floor, Children's Library Discovery Center, 2011.

The mini interactive displays and the nonfiction collection, Children's Library Discovery Center, 2011.

The fiction collections, Children's Library Discovery Center, 2011.

Exterior view of the new Children's Library Discovery Center, 2011.

Exterior view of the Central Library and the new Children's Library Discovery Center, December 2011.

Children's Library Discovery Center in Central Library, designed by 1100 Architect, has a total of 22,000 square feet, and is a $30 million building attached to the Central Library. It was the biggest urban children's library in the nation at the time of its construction. It is a state-of-the-art, interactive library, with features of a museum, classroom, and playground. Children (babies to age 12) and their caregivers can play, learn, and discover in this innovative space, with books, interactive exhibits, new technology, programs, and more.

Children's Library Discovery Center staff conducted "CLDC Mad Scientists" program, October 2011.

Children's Library Discovery Center robotic club, October 2011.

The Cat in the Hat program at Early Childhood Educational Center, Children's Library Discovery Center, September 2011.

STEM program/exhibit at the Children's Library Discovery Center, September 2011.

STEM program/exhibit, conducted by the Discovery Team, at the Children's Library Discovery Center, September 2011.

Children playing on computers in the mini cyber center in the Children's Library Discovery Center, October 2011.

Saturday Science Lab program, Children's Library Discovery Center, October 2011.

STEM program at the Children's Library Discovery Center, October 2011.

Kids playing in the Early Childhood Educational Center in the Children's Library Discovery Center, October 2011.

Halloween Party in Children's Library Discovery Center, November 2011.

In 2006, Central Library expanded its "Telephone Reference" to "Virtual Reference" by joining the OCLC "Question Point" 24/7 coop chat services. Networking with other libraries worldwide, with technical support by OCLC, customers could ask questions and chat online with librarians, 24/7, all year round.

Central Library Virtual Reference - providing online chats, emails, telephone and text services, 2009.

E: 2010s

In 2011, the Library started to renovate the Central Library public services areas after 45 years of services. Without closing the library, the renovation project was conducted phase by phase, while continuing to provide full customer services to the public.

Here is the Central Library renovation completion timeline:

Cyber Center	12/2011
Adult Service Areas	12/2012
Teen Space	10/2013
Central Circulation	08/2014
Main Floor Plaza	12/2015
Archives	08/2016

The poster announcing the renovation, 2011.

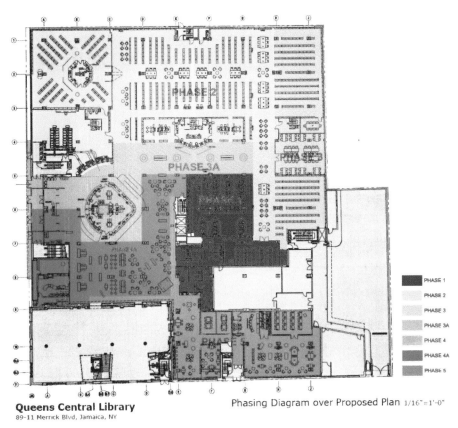

Queens Central Library
89-11 Merrick Blvd, Jamaica, NY

Phasing Diagram over Proposed Plan 1/16"=1'-0"

PHASE 1
PHASE 2
PHASE 3
PHASE 3A
PHASE 4
PHASE 4A
PHASE 5

The Central Library renovation plan, featuring 7 phases and conducted without closing the Library, 2010.

Business, Science & Technology Division and Social Science Division Reference Desk, before renovation, 2010.

The bookshelves and the reading areas, before the renovation, 2010.

The book displays, before the renovation, 2010.

Central Library under renovation, 2012.

Central Library under renovation, 2013.

The temporary circulation desk during the renovation, 2014.

The newly renovated Cyber Center, 2012.

The newly renovated Cyber Center, 2012.

The newly renovated Adult Reference Desk, Divisions reference service desks are integrated. 2013.

The newly renovated bookshelves, 2013.

The newly renovated reading areas, 2013.

The newly renovated book displays, 2013.

Part of the newly renovated Teen Space, October 2013.

The grand opening of the new Teen Space, December 12, 2013.

The newly renovated Central Circulation Services, December 2014.

Central Circulation Services – self-return stations, December 2014.

Central Circulation Services – Selfcheck-out stations, December 2014.

The new Media Center at Central Library after the renovation, December 2014.

The CD/DVD shelves and the services desk in the new Media Center at Central Library after the renovation, December 2014.

The new Central Café that is open to staff and the public, February 2015.

The magazine displays, December 2015.

The new quiet study room for adult readers, February 2015.

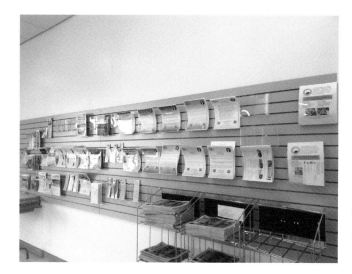

The community information bulletin board at Central Library, December 2015.

Central Library staff's work areas, December 2014.

During the renovation, the Central Library also changed its staffing structure completely. Subject divisions were eliminated, and librarians were pooled as one group but assigned into four cross-functional units: Collection Development, Programming and Outreach, Information Access Services, and Unique Services. Clerical staff were also be pooled to one unit under Central Library Circulation Services. Staff members were completely trained for the re-organization. At the same time, over 1.3 million materials in the Central Library, including public access materials and closed stacks materials, were re-organized by their Dewey Decimal Number, rather than subject matters. A climate–control storage was also built at the sub-basement for Archives to preserve archival materials in 2015.

Before the renovation, Central Library was divided into eight subject division. This picture taken in 2000 shows the eight divisions' managers: first line from left row, Alice Norris – Manager of Central Circulation Services, Nelson Yusheng Lu – Manager of Business, Science & Technology Division; Monica Rhodd – Manager of Social Science, & History Division, second row from left, Judith Todman, Manager of Long Island Division, Kathy Body – Manager of Literacy & Language Division, Lorna Rudder-Kilkenny, Manager of Information Services, Lynn Gonne, Manager of Children and Young Adult Services, and Esther Lee, Manager of Fine Arts & Recreation Division.

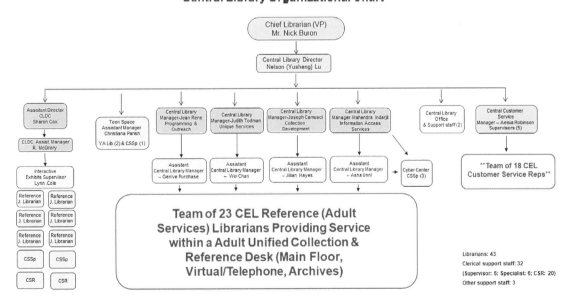

The new Central Library staff structure after renovation, 2018.

The main floor collection, arranged by Dewey Decimal number, 2015.

The closed stack collections, re-arranged by Dewey Decimal
number, 2016.

The new Archives, 2016.

Archives' map collection, 2016.

Children playing with the Dancing
Pendulum, Children's Library
Discovery Center, 2012.

Early Childhood Education program, 2012.

Central Library music performance by school students, November 2012.

Author talk and book signing program, November 2013.

Holiday season at the Teen Space, December 2013.

The Youth Counselor and the teens at the Teen Space, June 18, 2014.

Mother Goose program in the Early Childhood Educational Center, Children's Library Discovery Center, May 12, 2015.

Arts & Crafts program - celebrating Chinese Lunnar New Year (the year of Monkey), February 4, 2016.

In April 2016, Central Library celebrated the new Central Library in Merrick Blvd's 50th year of services. Central Library continues to provide variety of programs, activities and services to the communities.

The poster celebrating the new Central Library 50th Anniversary, April 20, 2016.

Proclamation, from Queens Borough President Melinda Katz, for Central Library, April 2016.

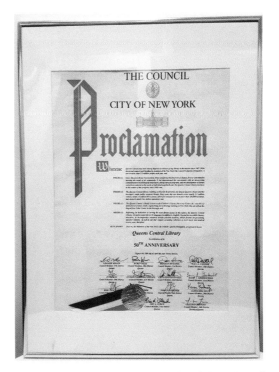

Proclamation, from the Council of the City of New York, for Central Library, April, 2016.

The "Birthday" cake for celebrating the new Central Library 50th Anniversary, April 20, 2016.

R & B artist Alexis Hightower 'right' performing to celebrate the new Central Library's 50th Anniversary, April 20, 2016.

Librarian Jeff Stephens (Central Library Manager - Collection Development) handling a large amount of donations, August 10, 2016.

Children playing with blocks at the Central Library annual Discovery Day street fair, September 10, 2016.

Central Library staff in a webinar training session, October 25, 2016.

"China-US Tourism Year 2016 Photography Exhibition" in Central Library, December 2016.

Chinese artists performing folk music to celebrate 2017 Lunar New Year at the main floor plaza, Central Library, January 23, 2017.

The broadcasting program for teens at the Teen Space, Central Library, March 23, 2017.

Summer Reading event at Central Library, June 8, 2017.

Central Library Chess Club, June 13, 2017.

NYC Legal Services at Queens Public Library, July 20, 2017.

Homework Help at Children's Library Discovery Center, October, 19, 2017.

"The Lion King" Broadway Show at Central Library, November 12, 2017.

Computer class for the public at the training room, Cyber Center, Central Library, November, 21, 2017.

Central Library became a Presidential Papers Depository Library, February 25, 2018.

QPL President & CEO Dennis Walcott and the audience in the "Southeast Queens Biannual: A Locus of Moving Points" opening ceremony, March 17, 2018.

Customers waiting outside the Central Library to get into the Library's program, June 14, 2018.

Customers watching the World Cup at the main floor plaza, July 3, 2018.

Central Library celebrating
Harry Potter's 20th
anniversary, July 31, 2018.

The Discovery Team in the
Discovery Day street fair,
September 8, 2018.

Central Library Annual Health
Fair, October 13, 2018.

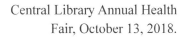

Special class/program for disability students, October 18, 2018.

Artist Patrick Killoran presenting his artwork "Passage" at Central Library, November, 10, 2018.

Hip Hop program at Central Library, December 26, 2018.

On April 2, 2019, Queens Library kicked off its "Renewed Promise to the Public" event, and changed its name from "Queens Library" to "Queens Public Library." The term renewal recognizes the 123-years of the Library's history, and that the library is constantly evolving to meet changing needs of the communities. The renewed promise to the public also means that there will be exciting changes in order to make absolutely clear "who we are, who we aspire to be, and how we will serve the public".

QPL President & CEO Dennis Walcott and former QPL staff Jimmy Van Bramer, Council Member of NYC, at the Renewed Promise to the Public kick-off event, April 2, 2019.

Central Library staff attending the Renewed Promise to the Public kickoff, April 2, 2019.

PART FOUR

The Future of the Central Library

The Queens Public Library system serves a population of 2.2 million through its Central Library and sixty-two branches. During FY 2018, Queens Public Library circulated a total of 12,413,013 items and welcomed more than 11,410,788 visitors. The Central Library circulated a total of 1,319,866 items and welcomed more than 1,439,544 visitors in the same FY year.

Central Library – a snapshot

	FY2017-18	Queens Library System-wide (FY2017-18)	CEL's Share of QL (FY2017-18)
Circulation	1,319,866	12,413,013	11%
Reference queries	158,857	1,132,201	14%
Chat sessions	5,193	--	--
Text messages	606	--	--
Computer sessions	268,991	2,172,247	12%
Program sessions	6,118	86,853	7%
Program attendance	125,946	1,506,969	8%
Read Down Your Fees	$11,863	$119,617	10%
Gate count	1,439,544	11,410,789	13%
Fines & Fees	$167,127	$1,277,926	13%
Customer's Request	156,520	802,487	20%
New card registrations	19,613	110,160	18%
New items added	69,657	512,280	14%
Holdings	1,192,526	4,972,428	24%
Non-library sponsored programs	1,076	--	--

Central Library FY 2018 snapshot.

Central Library has and will continue to play a vital role in the Queens Public Library system by providing free educational, informational, cultural, and recreational materials and services to the residents of the entire borough.

Central Library, with New York State Department of Taxation and Finance, offering free tax filing assistance for customers, January 30, 2017.

"What we've heard, what we can do" Great Jamaica Roadmap exhibition in Central Library, March 29, 2017.

Central Library participating in the Queens public Library is for Everyone campaign, April 26, 2017. From right to left: Joe Camusci, Central Library Manager - Collection Development, Judith Todman, Central Library Manager – Unique Services, Mahendra Indarjit, Central Library Manager – Information Access Services, and Nelson Yusheng Lu, Director – Central Library.

Arts & crafts program at Children's Library Discovery Center, June 8, 2017.

New York City First Lady Chirlane McCray visiting the Central Library to promote Thrive NYC initiatives, June 13, 2017.

Ms. Aeisia Robinson, Manager of Central Circulation Services, conducting a library card drive as an outreach activity, September 9, 2017.

Central Library monthly music salon, August 24, 2018.

Ms. Sharon Cox, Assistant Director of Children Library Discovery Center, and Ms. Brie Taylor, Children's Librarian, at the annual Discovery Day street fair, September 8, 2018.

An author talk in the auditorium, Central Library, September 12, 2018.

Youth Leadership Council program in the Teen Space, Central Library, January 03, 2019.

The Valenteens Day program in the Teen Space, February 13, 2019.

Central Library, with New York Historical Society, displaying the "Black Citizenship in the Age of Jim Crow" photo exhibition in the Black History Month, February, 2019.

Class visit at the Children's Library Discovery Center, Center Library, April 5, 2019.

Central Library Medical Librarian offering in-depth medical research assistance for customers every Wednesday, March 20, 2019.

Central Library has continued to be a leader in delivering information, new technology, and specialized services that meet identified community needs, as the following examples illustrate:

Book a Librarian – a library customer can make an appointment with Central Library so that a librarian will assist in his/her in-depth, special searching, or special needs.

Innovative Lab – A "worker space" that Central Library sets up to allow customer use of its 3-D printers, laser cutters, electronic sewing machines, and other technical devices.

Mobile Museum – Central Library purchased 12 pieces of adjustable displaying panels to display a variety of objects, including paintings and art.

Bloomberg Station – with support of Bloomberg Company, Central Library installed the Bloomberg Station, a comprehensive business and investment database, for public usage.

Culture Connection – A branded program established in Central Library which brings world-class performing arts and culture to the Library, showcasing the work of emerging artists and renowned masters.

Social Services – Alongside traditional services, Central Library introduced social services including help finding housing, domestic assistance, healthcare, job searching, and senior citizen services to the Library.

Customer filling the request through the website to "Book a Librarian" for in-depth, special research, 2018.

Librarians ready for the Book-A-Librarian in-depth reference services, 2019. From right to left: Jean Rene, Central Library Manager – Programming & Outreach, Mahendra Indarjit, Central Library Manager – Information Access Services.

A group of art students visiting the mobile museum at Central Library, August 15, 2018.

Haiti Cherie Exhibition at Central Library, May 2019.

The Bloomberg Company donated its Bloomberg Station to Central Library for customers, 2019.

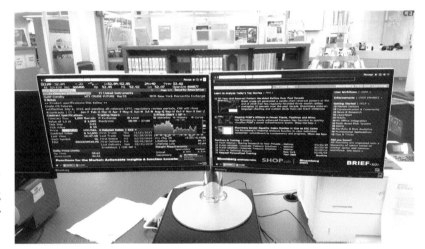

Culture Connection – Author Talk program, Mr. Dennis Walcott, President & CEO of QPL, interviewing Mr. Andre Aciman, New York Times bestselling author, about his book and film: "Call Me By Your Name". May 16, 2018.

Alton Fitzgerald White (Left), Broadway actor in The Lion King (role of King Mufasa), and Dayramir Gonzales (Right), artist from Havana, joining the Culture Connection program at Central Library, October 13, 2018.

Council for Airport Opportunity recruit customers to the workforce every Tuesday, 2019.

The flyer/poster for the new services at Central Library, 2018.

Mr. Nick Buron, Chief Librarian of QPL, got a flu shot at the plaza of the Central Library, with New York City Department of Health and Mental Hygiene, to promote vaccine awareness, October 25, 2018.

Since 2015, Central Library, with the Mayor's Office of New York City, has been the site of idNYC, offering New York City cards for all residents of New York City, 2019.

Throughout its history, from "Lighting the way", to "Enrich your life", to "We speak your language", the branded slogans of the Queens Public Library, the Central Library has innovated ways of serving the informational, educational, cultural, and recreational needs of the public, even as the borough itself has changed. The staff of Central Library, under the leadership of the Queens Public Library Administration and the Board of Trustees, have every expectation of continuing that tradition. Central Library will be as relevant in the future as it was in the past.

Queens Public Library: Everyone is Welcome Here.

Queens Public Library: We Speak Your Language.

Appendix

A: Directors/Chief Librarians/Presidents of Queens Public Library

Jessie Freemont Hume (Chief Librarian)	1907 – 1919
(Title of "Chief Librarian" was abolished in 1919, the new title of "Director" was established)	
John C. Atwater	1920 – 1925
Owen J. Dever	1925 – 1935
Elizabeth S. Radtke	1935 – 1936
(Title of "Director" was abolished in 1935, the title of "Chicf Librarian" was rc-cstablishcd)	
Louis J. Bailey (Chief Librarian)	1936 – 1954
Harold Tucker (Chief Librarian)	1954 – 1973
(Title was reverted back to "Director" during his tenure)	
John Solomita (Acting Director)	1973 – 1974
Milton Byam	1974 – 1979
Constance B. Cooke	1979 – 1994
Gary E. Strong	1994 – 2003
Thomas Galante (Interim Director)	2003 – 2005
(Director, President & CEO)	2005 – 2014
(Title changed to "President and CEO" during his tenure)	
Bridget Quinn-Carey (Interim President)	2014 – 2016
Dennis Walcott (President and CEO)	2016 –

B: Managers/Directors of Central Library, Queens Public Library

Caroline Crysler	1906 – 1908
Marcella Malone	1908 – 1926
Margaret S. Green (Reference Librarian)	1927 – 1934
Ethel Metzger (Acting Reference Librarian)	1935 – 1936
Jean K. Taylor (Chief Reference Librarian)	1937 – 1953
Charlotte E. Murray	1955 – ???
Ruth Grotheer	??? – ???
Essie Silverstein	??? – ???
Robert Cancienne	??? – ???
Orest J. Dutka	??? – ???
Charles Young	1976 – 1985
David Bosca	1987 – 1988
Carol Liu (Acting Manager)	1988 – 1988
Sherman Tang (Manager/Director)	1989 – 2000
Charles McMorran (Director)	2000 – 2001
Lorna Rudder – Kilkenny (Director)	2002 – 2009
Nick Buron (Associate Director)	2009 – 2012
Nelson Yusheng Lu (Assistant Director/Director)	2012 –

Acknowledgments & Credits

Many thanks to everyone involved in the completion of this book. Cynthia-Marie O'Brien, Copy Editor, Marketing & Communications, Queens Public Library, offered her great editing skills. Mrs. Judith Todman, Manager of Unique Services, Central Library, Queens Public Library, Mr. Ian Lewis, Senior Librarian, Archives at Queens Public Library, and Mr. Erik Huber, Senior Librarian, Archives at Queens Public Library, offered variety materials, suggestions and assistance in completing this project. Mr. Joseph Camusci, Manager of Collection Development, Central Library, Queens Public Library, offered some photographs that were selected in the book (Part Three, Section E) related to the Central Library's renovation project. Ms. Sharon Cox, Assistant Director, CLDC, Queens Public Library, and Mr. Robert McGrory, Former Assistant Manager, CLDC, Queens Public Library, also offered some photographs that were selected in the book (Part Three, Section D) related to the CLDC project. Ms. Mary Grace DeSagun, Digitization Supervisor, Technical Services, Queens Public Library, offered her assistance by scanning some photos from Archives collections.

Photographs in Part One, Part Two and portions of Part Three (Section A, B and C) were selected from Archives at Queens Public Library photograph collections. Historical information in this book (Part One, Section A) were mainly from Lighting the Way: The Centennial History of the Queens Borough Public Library 1896 – 1996, by Jeffrey A. Kroessler, Queens Library Foundation, Queens Public Library.

AUTHOR

Nelson Yusheng Lu was born in Guangzhou, China. After graduating from Zhongshan University, he decided to pursue new opportunities in America. He earned his M.A. in Asian Studies (1993) and M.L.S (1995) in St. John's University, New York. In November 1995, Nelson joined the Queens Public Library as General Librarian in the Business, Science & Technology Division at the Central Library. His career extended as he was promoted to Senior Librarian, Assistant Division Manager of Business, Science & Technology, Division Manager of Business, Science & Technology, Central Library Assistant Director, Director of Community Services and his current position as Director of Central Library. Nelson has been an integral force behind the Central Library's renovation/re-structure/re-organize projects during the 2010s. More resources, programs and better services are now provided to customers and to communities. Nelson is an active member of ALA, PLA and NYLA.

Nelson Yusheng Lu with his wife, Alice, now lives in Syosset, New York. He has two children – Larissa and Laurence.